Na Na Hey Hey Kiss Him Goodbye

Mary Rose Scinto

authorHOUSE®

AuthorHouse™
1663 Liberty Drive
Bloomington, IN 47403
www.authorhouse.com
Phone: 1-800-839-8640

© 2012 by Mary Rose Scinto. All rights reserved.

No part of this book may be reproduced, stored in a retrieval system, or transmitted by any means without the written permission of the author.

Published by AuthorHouse   06/28/2012

ISBN: 978-1-4772-2535-6 (sc)
ISBN: 978-1-4772-2536-3 (hc)
ISBN: 978-1-4772-2537-0 (e)

Library of Congress Control Number: 2012911085

Any people depicted in stock imagery provided by Thinkstock are models, and such images are being used for illustrative purposes only.
Certain stock imagery © Thinkstock.

Because of the dynamic nature of the Internet, any web addresses or links contained in this book may have changed since publication and may no longer be valid. The views expressed in this work are solely those of the author and do not necessarily reflect the views of the publisher, and the publisher hereby disclaims any responsibility for them.

Dedication

I would like to dedicate this book to my mom. I wish she was here to see and read this. I would also like to have my family share in this. A special thanks to my daughter Jenna for her photos and copies of photos in this book, including front and back covers.

A special thanks to Dale Frashuer and his family, rest in peace amigo. Also on this list Billy McLeain, Lionel (Link) Chamberlain, and Jerry Aiello. Miss you guys, we had a hell of a band.

Thanks to all the guys I had fun playing in the clubs and in the studio with. Dan Romo, Al Ferrante, David Spinosa, Ray Penn, Al Delmonte, Jeff Solomon, Pat Arvonio, Frank Salvo, Al Adams, Joey Melloti, and Clark Scheck. I would also like to thank Mike and McGee, Billy Vera, Richie and Dan at Al-Tel, Charles Rosenay, Edd Raineri, Joe Viglione, Joe Tortelli,

Jon Hichborn and Jan Jurgielewicz, who I know from years ago working the club circuit and has reentered my life working with me on some new projects. He is a great musician, friend and co-creator.

A very special thanks also to Mary Scinto for believing in me and wanting to get this story out.

If I left anyone out I apologize.

—Gary

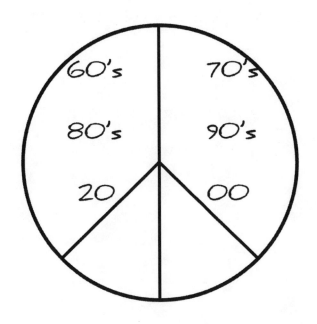

Let's Stroll
Thru Time
and
Salute The Artist
and
His Pop Culture
Hit
Of A Lifetime!

MRS

Contents

Na Na Hey Hey
Kiss Him Goodbye

Chapter 1

Gary's Childhood and Youth

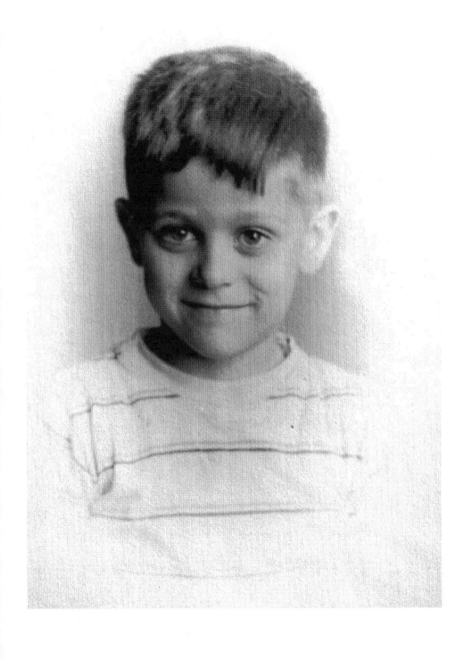

Gary's Childhood and Youth

It was in the eastern part of Connecticut in 1942 that a singer-songwriter was born. His name is Gary DeCarlo. He was born into a musical family. His mom sang, his father sang and played the guitar, and a sister who also sang. Gary was introduced to music at a very young age. He started out on the East side of Bridgeport until he was about seven years old. Prior to that his mom left his father when he was three. His dad was not ready to settle down with a family so the marriage ended. It was a very difficult time for them making ends meet with the rent, groceries, and over all expenses. Gary recalls that there were a few years that his sister and he had to wait until their mom received her income tax check to celebrate Christmas. According to Gary you just learned to accept things as they came but all in all we had fun and made the best of it. Gary and his family then went to live with his mother's friend Ann Gabriel. She had two children of her own, plus Gary, his mom, and his sister. They could not stay there for too long. They finally got an apartment on East Main St. It was a one-room apartment with a toilet in the hall. I could not understand at the time why my mother would always cry. Obviously, it is

8

hard for three people to live in one room apartments the size of a small bedroom. Gary's grandmother on his father's side got the family and apartment on the second floor, right under hers. It was two rooms but at least they could go upstairs and eat meals with her. This has helped Gary's family so much at that time. Gary's own mother was a kind, caring and giving woman. She would give her last dollar. She had a pretty rough life when she was young. Her mother passed away when she was seven years old. She was pulled out of school to raise Gary's uncles and aunts. Gary says that this is why she loved having the family get-together on all the holidays. For his mother not even completing elementary school she could hold her own in different situations. Gary's mom had a nice sense of humor, and was a very warm and kind woman.

The family finally moved to the hollow section of Bridgeport when he turned eight years old. Gary explains that the house was condemned. The outside of the home was cracked and splintered from neglect over the years. The electricity was not to be believed. If you changed a fuse sparks would fly like Fourth of July. There were rats in the basement large enough to ride. In the winter months just sitting in the living room you could see the drapes blow away from the window each time the wind would blow.

This was a six family house and the landlord owned the factory next door. Even though the home was condemned the city would not take the home down. His mom at the time paid $24 a month. Gary remembers that their apartment was pretty shabby being that it was used for a store room and it was vacant for a long time. At that point Gary, his mom, and his sister did not have very many places to go that they could afford. Remember, it was a very difficult time for them and this was their only option. Gary's uncle reassured his mom that they would fix up the apartment and they did in time. The family had to share bathroom facilities out the back hall. They had problems with the facilities all the time. Then Gary's uncle installed in his apartment a toilet, hot water tank, and a small shower because remember it was a cold water flat. That was how a good portion of apartments where in that time.

Gary was very active in sports when he went to school on the west end of Bridgeport. When Gary went to high school he played football believe it or not. His size did not stop him from doing the things he wanted to do. Because of his size he got a lot of weird looks especially when he came down to sign up. When Gary tried out the coach at the time Ed Riley had him run 100 yard sprints. He thought he was going to die. On that day he recalls he was about to give up. He met a friend

Bobby Ventrasca who said to him, don't give up now Gary, you can do it. So he did not give up and the coach told him to run out and make a few catches, which he did. He then told Gary to buy a pair of shoes because he was going to dress for the first varsity game. Gary was first string junior varsity and second string varsity. He recalls he was thrilled. He never forgot what Bobby said to him. They became friends for some time. Unfortunately he does not see him that often but he still regards him as a good friend.

Gary says that the funny part of this is that he was 5'3" tall so he could leave his equipment anywhere because no one else could fit into them. His size did not stop him from doing the things he wanted to do. Whatever he pursued he packed a powerful punch and was great at it. As he was growing up, Gary always love to dance any chance he could, and with his musical family that was quite often. With all the stress he had to endure growing up the family loved music and that music was a major role in keeping them happy and alive. All in all what Gary had to deal with as a child his God given talent shined through and his interest into music became stronger and stronger. He had no idea what a gift he had and what his life would become in the music industry.

Gary's sister Marie would bring him to the CYO dances at the local church. He recalls they would play records and he would dance the bop with his sister and her friends. In the 50's this was a favorite pastime of the young kids. The dances went on at the Ritz ballroom. Gary, his sister Marie, and her friends would dance the night away. He remembers that the people would make a circle around him and his group. They were amazed and they could not stop watching the kid in the one powder blue button pegged pants suit dance. Gary was going on 10 and his talent in music was starting to shine through.

When Gary lived on Oak Street he started to rollerskate at a rink that was located on State Street in Bridgeport Connecticut. It was called the Mosque. He had met new friends along the way and he went to the rink with his cousin Nicky Gagliardi, Pat Frasher, Tony Cavalli, and sometimes with Louie Gay when he was home on leave from the Navy. They went to the rink often so he became a pretty good skater. Gary's cousins and his friends were older than him and they would tell people that Gary was 12. Really! Gary says, like that would make such a difference. About a year or two had passed and he began to skate with a female partner. They then entered into several competitions. It was great Gary recalls and they even took home a few trophies. When Gary was about 12 or 13 in 1954/1955 his favorite pastime was to sit by the radio and listen to Alan Freed on a show called Moon dog. When I first heard the show I could not believe how much I liked it, Gary said. It was so cool, and very different, from the show tunes and the other stations.

The Five Satins, The Moonglows, The Flamingos, Little Richard, Jerry Lee Lewis, to name a few. Gary was determined to be a singer. He recalls that every night he would lay in bed and say to himself he hopes someday to get a nice voice and to be able to sing and live his dream. According to Gary he was hooked on American Bandstand. He would watch the show and sing-along. His dream was someday to be on that show.

Chapter 2

The Gift of Music Begins

The Gift of Music Begins

Gary would go to the record hops and shows at the Ritz ballroom and pleasure Beach ballroom, always singing and hoping he would get better.

Back in that time Thursday nights were a big night to walk or Cruise the "Main Drag" as it was called! You would walked down one side of Main Street to John Street turn around and come back on the other side basically until all the stores closed at 9 PM. Remember there were "NO MALLS". This was just a quaint little new England town. Gary said we would meet all our friends and we were introduced to new friends along the way. This is where Gary first met Paul. He said they would run into each other and say hi, also they would see each other at record hops and other music events. The guys in the crowd that Gary hung around with did not want to sing. A few times he tried to get it together but it did not work out, so again his singing career was still just a dream. As Gary got a little older he would visit his sister at her house and she would have Johnny Mathis records on the stereo. He could not stop listening to the songs. Gary would play them over and over again till he knew every song. Then one night he was in a club, somehow it came up that he wanted to be a singer. The band that was playing that night invited Gary up on stage to sing. He says; I bet you cannot guess what songs I chose to sing that night? Yes—Johnny Mathis, I chose three songs that I was hooked on he said, and those three songs I practiced over and over and over again. That was Gary's first shining moment. Now he was HOOKED! His singing career was about to begin.

Rudy would take Gary to his gigs and he would just sit there all night watching and listening and taking it all in. He would also take him to the club on Dixwell Avenue in Hamden Connecticut.

Gary recalls dancing at that time to the two-step or bop. His cousin Rudy Mobilio played the drum and his brother Al played the Piano. They were into jazz and they were great! Rudy knew Gary showed an interest into playing the drums so when he was able to buy a new set he then gave the old set to Gary. Needless to say Gary was thrilled. They set up the drums set in the living room and Gary recalls in the warmer months when we opened the windows the people in the neighborhood could hear him play. There was a park cross the street and people would shout "GO GARY GO". Gary's adventure into music was on his way.

Rudy's influence in music brought Gary to a new level in his journey. According to Gary he said that he will never forget Rudy and what he did for him with his music and his generosity.

Gary's adventure into music was on its way. He also played the drums for the eighth and ninth grade graduation class.

Unfortunately Gary quit school at the end of his 10th year. He felt that there was something better out there for him. Gary said that he did not regret quitting school but he knows now that he should have least finished high school. His first job was when he turned 12 years old. The job was setting pins up at the Pequonnock bowling alleys. Gary was not as fast as the others doing this job due to a lower back problem, which he found out later that he had broken his tailbone as a kid. He had a goal getting this job, it was a red Ryder BB Rifle. Gary recalls when he got his first paycheck he was about to go and buy the red Ryder when he remembered that his mom's birthday was coming up. He went downtown with his sister Marie and after all he bought his mom of very special gift with his money. It was a black and gold teapot that looked like an Aladdin lamp. She loved it and kept it for years until she passed away.

Gary now has that teapot as a remembrance of his mom.

Chapter 3

Composing, Singing, Recording

Dick Alexander, Teeners Aid
Mental Health Fund Campaign

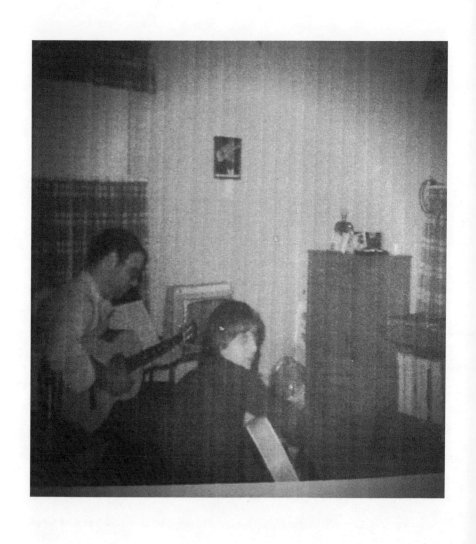

CANADA LOUNGE
EVERY FRIDAY and SATURDAY
Presents

THE MIGHTY ORCHIDS
Featuring

GARY DEE
Exit 10, Off New England Thruway
690 MAMARONECK AVE. — AMPLE PARKING
Telephone for Reservations — OWens 8-5780

NITECLUBS   COLLEGES   PARTIES

Music for All Occasions
THE FABULOUS

Orchids

featuring GARY DEE
The biggest and most exciting sound around
Please call —
LIONEL CHAMBERLAND   838-0702
                                             (Norwalk)

GARY DeCARLO   366-1927
                                             (Bridgeport)

Composing, Singing, Recording

It was in 1958 that Gary moved to Pequonnock Street in Bridgeport. At that time he was still very much into music. He recalls that he was always buying 45's listening to the music, and dreaming of his success someday.

Gary met a couple of new guys in town. Joe Reed, Dale Frashuer, Johnny Castle and Frank Borrelli. When he turned 16 he then became a member of their Doo Wop Group. This was Gary's time to branch out into the world of music. He recalls going into New York in 1959 making their first record of the song; "That's The Way It Will Be/Elaine". The label was Jubilee Records. FYI; Gary was notified that this song could be purchased on the Internet.

The group was called "The Glenwoods" then. Our second record was "Summers Here (School Is Thru)" Gary said. They were the "Chateaus" at the time. The record label was Coral Records. This all took place one or two years later.

Gary mentioned that he became involved as a single artist with a few bands that were already mentioned in previous writings. Then Gary said he hooked up with the "Orchids" a seven piece horn group that was quite good. This all happened around 1963/1964 and Gary stayed with them until my 1967.

In the early to mid-60's Gary was singing with the "Orchids" at a club in Mamaroneck New York. The club was called The Canada Lounge. During Gary's sets on stage he recalls that he would announce the name of the songs they were about to do. Every few weeks or so he would announce "Hey Girl", and a girl in the audience would jump out of her seat and announced her approval. Eventually Gary met that girl and was immediately attracted to her. He said to me, you know how when you meet someone you can tell that you're right for each other. Unfortunately she did not come to the club as often as he would have liked her to. She just lived a great distance away. She would come to the club with her friends and she was very devoted to them.

They began to talk to each other at the club and also on the phone and he became aware that she had two young sons. That made it even harder for us to see each other, he said. As time went by Gary started to care for her very much, but because of the amount of alcohol and pills that he was doing he was not thinking very clear at the time. Gary went to see her one night and because of the condition he was in the visit did not turn out very well. When he called her the next day she was very cool towards him which really bummed him out. Needless to say this situation did not help him with the drinking and the pills he was taking. This all caused Gary to become more depressed. As time went by Gary left the band and cleaned up his act, going into New York City.

Gary had seen her one last time at a club in Banksville, N.Y. We had about 3 to 4 hours together that night, he recalls, they had a few laughs. Gary did ask her why she had come to this club which he was going to on the weekends. But, her friends came over and told her they were leaving. Gary said goodbye. He did not even ask her if she wanted to stay with him. He said to me, I would have taken her home that night. Something Gary deeply regrets. Gary tried to give her space and the night went by so quick, and the opportunity slipped out of his hands. That was the last time Gary would ever see or talk with her again. He does not even know if she ever knew that it was him singing on the record. Because of what happened with Paul, believe me, he said, I had put everything into singing the song that night, hoping that one day he would see her and tell her about the record and tell her he was singing the song to her.

Some time had passed and Gary found out through friends that she moved to Arizona with her boys and sadly passed away.

All in all Gary remembered and cherished the time they spent together and he would never forget that very special girl he met, who was in the audience, jumping out of her seat, to give her approval to the song and "Hey Girl".

Gary and his family moved again to Laurel Avenue in 1960. Again they moved to the corner of Norman Street and Laurel Avenue in 1961 where they lived for two years. This is the house where he would visit his sister on the first floor and begin listening and singing to Johnny Mathis records. Then in 1965 Gary and his family moved to Federal Street in the North end of Bridgeport till about 1972. At that time Gary recalls he had bought a small keyboard with cord buttons on it and began to write more songs. He told me that he rehearsed in their garage with a few bands, but had to stop due to the neighbors complaints. Some of the people in the bands were Billy McCleain, Danny Romo, David Spinose, Al Delmonte, Jerry Aiello, Barry Marshall, Al Ferrante, Joey Millotti, and a few more names than escape them at the moment. Gary apologizes to those he did not mention.

He was living here when he had started going into New York in 1968. At that time Gary bumped into Paul Leka at Buddah Records. "NA NA" as he called it was recorded in the month of June in the year 1969 and he is pleased to say that the song went to number one in the country and the top 10 in almost every country in the world. The song stayed number one for two weeks. He could not believe this at the time but the "NA NA" song bumped the Beatles out of number one with their two-sided hit "Come Together and Something".

Gary said to me with much emotion; "if the Beatles could put two A-Sides together on one record why then did they not allow me to do it"? It worked for the Beatles why not for me, he asks?

The family stayed in their home for seven years until Gary purchased a multi family house in the west end of Bridgeport. Gary recalls that he would have many musicians and friends over his house for jamming sessions all night long. Music was his passion. He would eat—sleep—and breath into his world of music.

Gary decided he wanted a piano to add to his studio, so he purchased an electric piano and housed it into his outside attic with amps and recording equipment. He still found the need for a piano for his apartment, so he called around and found one in Wilton Connecticut. The piano was an old upright from England, circa 1870. Gary said that he had to have it tuned into concert pitch. He said that he made up his mind that he had to improve and get much better playing the piano so he could then make demos to send and bring with him to New York and California. Gary and his brother in law Al, went to pick up the piano and bring it home, however in addition they needed to hire two piano movers as well. The four guys carried the Piano up to the third floor.

After much diligence and many frustrating attempts Gary was finally able to put cords together and write songs. He was determined to do this, Gary told me that he was not a piano player by no means, but he could punch out rhythms, and melody lines that were not bad. In fact they were quite good. He was able to start putting songs on tapes and showing his work. He then began to make demo tapes getting a little better each time. Gary recalls that he had spent his last $2500 on four songs and recorded them in Bridgeport.

Gary then wound up on United artist records. The record company flew him to California and that is where he recorded the songs in 1975. The song titles were "Tommrow Is Another Day and I Fall In Love Again". Stephen Madeo, Stevie Wonder's trumpet player and arranger from WonderLove was on the session with Niecy Williams and a few other real good singers and musicians. They each came out but did not get a lot of exposure. Being sandwiched between Paul Anka and War did not help. Gary said that he thought they were good but they did not make the top 40.

Not too long after this Gary received a call from his lawyer/ manager and he asked Gary if he would like to go down to

Muscle Shoals Alabama to cut some of his songs. He said yes, and they flew him down there. Boy were his arms tired, ha ha. Anyway, he recorded a few songs and he had met several people who were so nice. It was such a pleasure to be there Gary said. When he returned to New York after some time he received a phone call from the very same people. They asked Gary if he would consider moving down there and to continue working with them. Unfortunately, because of where his head was at the time, he declined. Gary knows he should have taken the chance and gone.

When Gary set up his apartment on Poplar Street he put speakers in all of the rooms so he could hear music no matter where he was. Gary said that it was great to take a shower or bath surrounded by music and low lighting. Music had a special magical effect on me, he recalls. Plain and simple; it was a mood elevator!

Gary however noticed that if he was in a down mood he could write sensitive ballads. He told me that he would much prefer up beat rhythms that everyone could dance to. Music was the profession Gary had chosen and also his fantastic hobby. I find at times it is a little difficult to compose songs because of what happened with "NA NA", Gary says. He has to take off the headset and shut all the music down because it makes him so anxious. He also said that he even had to stop watching all those shows like American Idol because of all the negative comments throughout the program. Gary tells it to me with such emotion; "No one knows what it is like to get up on stage to bear your heart and soul and perform the best that you can". He said it is as if all of your nerve endings are exposed, and it is the same when you write a song. They are like your children he said, some are good, and some are not, but to constantly be turned down when you know that the songs are good is not easy to take. He expressed how all of the negativity does quite a number on your confidence. But all in all you must keep going, to achieve your goal. Gary used to tell people that they rolled the A & R guys which is the Artist Repetire men's names with chalk, on their doors, so it would be easy to erase. Most of them did not last for very long. They had the attitude that if they say NO to your song, most of the time they would be right. So they did not have to worry about their job, as long as the higher ups did not find out that they passed on a potential hit.

Gary was sitting on his sofa one day and it finally sunk in that he did not have any new connections or ways to make it work. The people that Gary had met over the years were either retired or dead or had gone onto a greater glory. He recalls that these people would not even talk to him when he called them. The names like Tommy Matolla, Irv Azoff, Jimmy Iner, to name a few. Gary remembered that he sat there and he could feel the emptiness that he could not describe. He said it was as if he was an empty shell on a lonely beach. He could not believe that he had a #1 Hit Record but he was treated as if he was a second-class citizen. Gary felt at that point no one cared and he felt like the biggest loser on the planet. He said that what was eating him inside is that he always felt that he would get a second chance.

Then in 1977 the organ player from the Chicago White Sox started to play the "NA NA" song at their games. The fans really got into it and it then became their team song. Each time a pitcher was relieved or winning they would sing the song. Now Gary was starting to feel a little bit better, the light was beginning to shine a little through the tunnel.

The year that the Yankees won the World Series the "NA NA" song was used on CD and DVD, "The Dream Team". The song was also used in past years when President Bush left office and boarded his helicopter, hundreds of people standing in front of the Washington Monument sang "Na Na" as he flew away. The song would also be used by Hallmark in their greeting cards, even with sound. The "Na Na" song became to be used by just about every team in the sporting arenas. Football, hockey, soccer, you name it, they used it!"

In 1987 "NA NA" was recorded by a Doo Wop Group called the "Nylons" from Canada. The song went to # 12 on the national charts. It was also used on just about every sitcom show, on TV starting from Cheers to date, and the list goes on. Several commercials by Budweiser, Miller light, Nissan, Koehler, Tide-To-Go, again just to name a few.

As far as films it was used in the movie "Eddie" with Whoopi Goldberg, "Remember The Titans" in 2000 with Denzel Washington and "Raising Helen" with Kate Hudson.

In 2009 Gary had four records out using the "Na Na" chant. Christina DeBarge had "Goodbye" out, Wale Rapper from Washington DC had one called "Chillin with Lady Gaga". Jay Z had it on a song called "Death Of An Auto Tune" and a record called "We Ready" which is also being played at sporting events.

In 2010 Gary received a call from a guy named Frank Deluca and he asked him if he would consider doing a show on PBS with many other singers and groups from the 50's and 60's. Gary immediately said yes and arrangements were made for him to fly to Pittsburgh Pennsylvania. Gary brought his wife Annette and older daughter Jenna to this event. The light was beginning to shine brighter at the end of the tunnel. Words cannot express how Gary felt at that moment. This was a very busy weekend at the show in Pittsburgh PA. They had 59 acts coming in. There was a Friday, Saturday, and Sunday show. It was on May 22, 2010 Benedum Theatre in Pittsburgh PA. Gary felt so at home on stage performing that he could hardly wait for that day to come. Gary recalls that he had a really great time performing and meeting all the talented

41

artists and performers who have been in the business since the 50's and the 60's. What really blew Gary's mind that day was that many of the fans wanted to have pictures taken with him and wanted his autograph. Even the staff, they could have not been nicer to him.

He waited a year and a half for the show to air. It finally aired on December 3, 2011. The show was called the 60s pop rock soul (My Music). The show was produced by a guy named T.J. Lubinsky whose company is called My Music and partnered with PBS. Gary again explained that the thing that blew his mind was the head of the show called Gary, "A Legend" because the song had spanned over so many decades. Each person that Gary spoke to had a happy story to tell. At the time "NA NA" was out Gary tried to project a good feeling in his vocals on the record. That was a great time in Gary's life something he will never forget!

When Gary did the show in Pittsburgh for TJ and Henry DeLuca, he did not do it for the money. Gary did the show for the exposure and for the love of singing and performing.

In October 2010, he received a call from a guy named Charles Rosenay asking him if he would consider singing at the Beat Expo convention in Stamford Connecticut with Julie Grant, Tommy Roe, Juma Sultan, Ian Lloyd and The Mersey

Beat. Gary said yes he would perform with great pleasure. It took place on November 27, 2010. He had a blast doing the show. Again Gary had people wanting to take pictures with him and for him to sign autographs. The next day was the Expo, that is where he sat under a poster with his picture on it and the name of the record.

Gary was interviewed by three people that night, including Edd Raineri, who has a radio show in PA called Beatledd. Guess who it is about? Edd and Gary hit it off and became friends. He is a cool guy Gary said. He has had Gary on his show a few times via telephone and also put articles and pictures on his Facebook page of him.

In October 2011, Gary received an e-mail from Edd asking him if he would do a benefit performance for show in Wilkes-Barre Pennsylvania. This benefit was for the people who lost their homes and possessions from a hurricane, that caused major flooding and damage in their area. Gary told him that he would come and sing for the families as well as anyone else in the Wilkes-Barre area near Scranton. It was about 3 1/2 hours one way. Gary was performing at the Genitti Hotel which was very nice and the hotel had a large room to perform in. There were two bands performing that night. Each band was a big draw from previous years and this was the first time they had ever been on the same stage together. Gary did a quick rehearsal and then prepared to perform. 1000 people showed up that day. The hotel had to open the entire room which was pretty large due to the outpouring of people. The show was great and all the people were there to have a good time. When Gary came off the stage a man came up to him with his wife and said that the "Na Na" song was his favorite song. He proceeded to tell Gary that in 1969 he was in Vietnam and the people from his squad as well as himself would huddle around the radio and listen for "Na Na" to come on. And when they all heard it, they knew they would, come home safe from their mission. Gary with the much emotion replies; "WOW" That Gave Me The Chills! He thanked him very much, they took a few pictures together and they said their goodbyes.

Gary recalls that several people approached him to take pictures and asked him to sign autographs as well. One man came up to Gary with two 45's of "Na Na" and asked him to autograph them. He also said to me that it was his favorite record. About two weeks later Gary received a thank you letter from the Red Cross chapter in that area. The letter said that the show was a success and it brought in a good amount of money. Gary told me that this was a great experience for him and a memorable one that touched his heart and soul.

Gary recalls during his life growing up and listening to many styles of music his favorite being R & B Blues. He said they were great over the years and had inspired him. Here are a few artist that he recalls; James Brown, Ray Charles, José Feliciano, Tower of Power, Average White Band, Michael McDonald, Phil Collins, Foriegner, Grand Funk Railroad, Marvin Gaye, just to name a few. All of these artists have loved what they did for a living and were proud of their accomplishments. Consumate professionals! Gary tried to do that mindset every time he performed and he was told by quite a few people that he was very good. If something had happened musically for Gary where he had gone on the road, he would have asked Rudy to be his drummer, of course Gary explains that he is talking about after "Na Na ". Let us say around mid-70's into 80's.

Gary recalls having a lot of memories from the house on Poplar St. In Bridgeport. He would come down and have coffee with his mother and read the newspaper. Every Sunday he recalls his mother would make a large pot of sauce and fry up the meatballs with sausage which you could smell through the entire house, I might add. This would be our Sunday ritual while reading the newspaper and having fresh coffee. Ah, the good old days! Gary's mother loved to have company so she would always invite his uncles and their wives, and Gary's sister, his niece and nephews for all of the holidays. He recalls they would sit around the table and eat and just have fun. Gary's mother felt the more the merrier. She loved to cook and see all of us enjoy the meal and each other's company. Eventually Gary's sister and her husband Al bought a house in Naugatuck Connecticut but would still come to moms for the holidays. Just about every picture in those days were taken with all of the family sitting at the dining room table. As the years passed Gary's sister Marie's children all have found spouses and married. Gary's niece Gina married Louie Gabriel. Gary always considered him his blood nephew. He also became Gary's best friend in the years to come. Then in the 80's and early 90's Gary would go with his wife Annette to their house in Waterbury Connecticut they were and still are very generous and a lot of fun to be with, Gary says. They would have cookouts for certain holidays and just for getting together with family. Louie and Gary became closer each time. They both love music and like to laugh. According to Gary unfortunately nothing is off limits. Sometimes we laugh till our faces hurt. Louie is a great cook and loves to cook on the grill so naturally Louie and his son Zach started a business which Gary says he hopes they do extremely well with. Gary's niece Gina is a creative person, she does the hair and makeup for weddings and photo shoots. She also makes great jewelry. Gary expresses how happy he is to have the relationship he has with them and hopes that it continues forever just to be at their house at times Gary says, helped him through a few rough patches.

In the early months of 2010 Gary received his first call from Henry DeLuca and that he told him he had called Paul and that Paul told him he was no longer involved with music and to call Gary because he sang the original record Gary said that he cannot emphasize how it hurt him not to be able to go out and perform this record. He knows if he had done this he would have had a few more records released. They might not have equaled "Na Na" but who knows we could have gotten more mileage out of it, he said. Gary explains that he cannot stress the fact that he cannot get all of those years back or his youth. But he says at this point in his life he is having a slight hearing problem, but that does not stop him, he still loves to write, sing, and perform. Gary says he does not know if he could do any lengthy touring. Maybe he said if he had a press agent or if he had support from local newspapers and or radio stations, but that has not happened and he is still waiting for it to happen in this date and time. Gary feels that he has done something that few people in the music industry have done. He has spanned into the late 60's, 70's, 80's, 90's, into 2012 and it is still going strong, "Thank God".

Please do not get the wrong idea about me Gary says. I am not always feeling sorry for myself or down Gary explains that if you meet him you could see for yourself. He is not looking for sympathy, but as he puts it, "I Want What Was Rightfully Mine", so when the time comes and I can close my eyes knowing I had made a contribution and also make people sing and dance to my songs and music.

In the early 70's Gary met a producer by the name of Ted Cooper who had a hit at the time with "Elephant's Memory". Ted and Gary hit it off and began to look for material to record. Ted was a friend of Carol Kings. He played for Gary some cuts from an album she had made with her husband Jerry Goffin. Ted recorded "To Love" with Gary. Jerry Goffin and Carol, unfortunately were getting a divorce, so this album did not get the right exposure. He liked the song called "Ma Ma is Uncle Clayton Jackson Sleeping Here Tonight". This song was written by Tony Wine and Irwin Levine. As you can tell by the title it was very controversial. When the song came out on the radio, stations would not play it, claiming it was too suggestive. Ted then played Gary an album by a guy named James Taylor. It had been sitting on a shelf in record stores and not selling. Gary had no idea why, to him there was nothing wrong with that version. So Ted and Gary went looking for something else to record. He would go to Ted's place and sing as he would play the piano. Ted lived in a castle that had been converted into several apartments. Gary explained that the natural sound in the room was excellent. As time went by unfortunately Ted became ill. His condition worsened and sadly he passed away. Gary then met Irwin Levine and Larry Brown who had just written a song called "Candida". They would go on to write a string of hits for "Tony Orlando and Dawn". They were very busy with that project so Irwin introduced Gary to the producer, whose name was Hank Medress. Hank and Gary hit it off pretty good. He really liked my voice, Gary said. When they would go over a song at the piano now he would say, "Look at that he just opened his mouth and it comes right out". Gary recorded one song with Hank. He put his voice on track to a song called "Rescue Me". It was originally done by Fontilla Bass. Unfortunately it was not done in Gary's key and was never released. At the same time Irwin wanted him to record a song called "Smokeys

Place" which was another redo. They had brought in Charlie Calello to produce it again, it never came out. Gary was in the studio doing something for Hank. Charlie was there that day and said that he liked his voice and wanted to do something with him. After some time had passed Gary did not hear from Charlie. They told Gary that he had gone to the mountains to find himself. Gary did not know if that was true or a line, but at the time he would have believed anything. A few years later he had made a record, with Englebert Humperdink called "After The Lovin" which was a big hit. After several months Gary received a phone call from Hank Medress asking him if he would like to be in a group he wanted to start along with him and Ellie Greenwich. Gary turned him down because he had just signed with a lawyer in New York and the lawyer was showing a tape that Gary recorded in Bridgeport, which was put out on United artist label. Gary explained to me how hard it is to make someone understand how many times you get smacked down, told no, and just plain ignored in the business. He said you just have to pick yourself up and say to yourself okay I got to keep going and reach my goal. First and foremost you cannot allow all of this to get in the way of your creativity. He said that is a little easier when you are younger but it gets harder as you get older due to the amount of pressure on you for bills, mortgage, kids, tuition, etc. Gary had a small slipcover business back then. He had to go to the customer's home and pin-fit the fabric to the existing furniture, take it home and finished the job. This type of business helped and allowed Gary to still go into New York and pursue his dream, which at times was feeling out of reach.

When Gary was 16 he met a bunch of guys at a burger place called Briarwood's on the corner of North and Boston Ave. This is where Gary met Dale, Joe, and John. Joe and Gary would get together a lot, as a matter of fact he recalls, we would work at the same auto parts store. Gary delivered and Joe was the counterman. Joe told him he was in a singing group with Dale and John and that a guy named Dennis was leaving the group. Joe knew how much Gary loved to sing and that he wanted to be in a group, so he told the guys in the group about him. Gary said we all met and he sang the top end in the harmony. He could not have been happier. So John, Frank, Dale, Joe, and Gary are a "Doo-Wop Group". They all rented an office on East Main St. in Bridgeport and rehearsed five nights a week 7 to 11 after we would go to Briarwood and hang out. One of the streets down in that area was Glenwood Avenue, hence the first name of the group was "The Glenwoods", second name was "The Citations", the third name was "The Chateaus". The group had a few records out at that time, the song "That's The way It Will Be Elaine", on Jubilee records. "Summers Here (School Is Out)" which Gary wrote when he worked at the parts store. The group and Gary were in the midst of a contract problem and it was suggested that they put the songs in other people's names mainly to protect the writers from having a problem. Then when the matter was cleared the real writers would then get the credit. Regretfully, Gary admits that he was not savvy at the time to the legal side of the business. As it all turns out Gary says, that it was put in Paul's name, yes Paul's name, and another guy named Nick Dillolio who was acting as manager. Gary explained; now let me back up just a little bit. As a Doo-Wop Group we were putting together a book of songs that we did. It all totaled 150 songs. We had dance routines he said for all of them as well.

One day Paul's name came up. They would do some Shows and Paul had a group also, so they would see each other a lot. Gary and his group found out that he was playing piano now and wanted to be a piano player. Naturally Gary and the guys said yes and they hauled his piano up a flight of very steep stairs. Gary said that it is how Paul's name came to be on their record as a writer for my song, which he proudly displayed on his wall, never telling anyone mind you that "I WROTE IT"!

A year or two later Dale told Gary and the guys that Paul asked him to go to New York with him and try to get in the music business that way. He had first met Bob Reno and I guess he liked what he had to say. Naturally the group broke up, but Gary and the guys managed to get quite a few singing jobs before they did which went over very well. After that Gary was in several bands and one more group called "Gary And The Coachman". The bands were "C.C. Davis, Denny And The Dynatones, The Checkmates and Gary's favorite "The Orchid's. As "The Orchids" they played all the local clubs, plus the Country House aka The Deercrest Inn in Banksville, N.Y. The Canada Lounge in Mamaroneck New York, the Lakeview Inn, the Cheetah in New York City, Yale, Princeton, Dartmouth, and Sacred Heart University. The Cheetah wanted Gary and his group on a regular basis but the guys in the band were mostly married, had kids, or were starting a family so they all said no. Gary recalls that he was devastated. This band was great he said and he thought that they were going places. Not so long after this he gave his notice and moved on. Gary started in a few bands with his drummer and good friend Billy McLeain. What Billy did, Gary said, on a skimpy set of drums, you would not believe! You would have to hear it for yourself. He was "Funk" Gary says. He misses him. Sadly he passed away. He misses (Link) Lional Chamberlain who in his estimation was one of the best guitar players he has ever heard. "Rest In Peace Guys".

Gary took a few months off trying to get his head together. He finally decided that he was going to record something, going to New York City with the demo, and sell it! Back at that time Gary said, you could go door to door. So this is exactly what he did. He went to 1650 Broadway the Brill Bldg. and he went floor to floor. At that time there were small label producers etc. in those buildings. Gary went into Buddah Records and who does he say sitting at a desk but "Paul"! They talked for a while and he asked what he was doing. Gary told him he had put out something and that he was looking for a label. Paul introduced Gary to Bob Reno.

Chapter 4

The Truth Behind the Na Na Song

COMING SOON!

One of the most
fantastic records I
have ever heard. No
hype, no nonsense —
this will be one of the
biggest records of 1969!

"NA NA HEY HEY
(KISS HIM GOODBYE)"

Watch for it soon on

Fontana records

NA NA HEY HEY KISS HIM GOODBYE

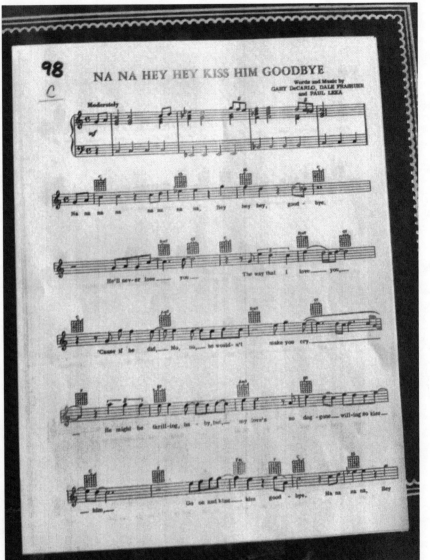

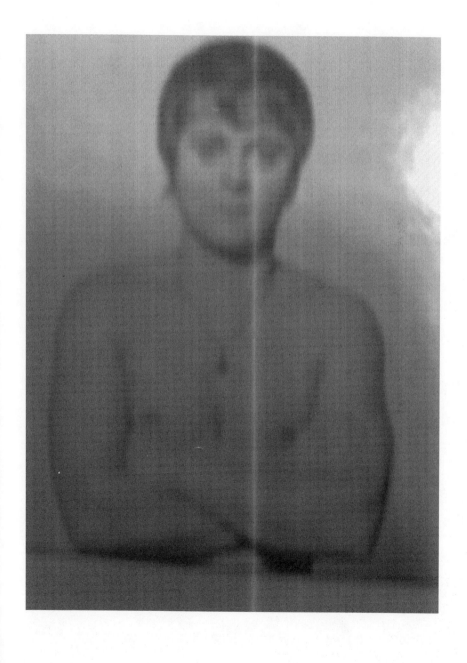

The Truth Behind the Na Na Song

After that Gary started to go into New York City on a regular basis. Paul and Gary started to be together a lot. He told Gary that Bob became vice president of Mercury records in New York and that he (Paul) would be getting an office, a secretary, and an office to write and practice in. Paul would take Gary to rehearsals, recording studio sessions, and meetings. Gary would sit on the couch in Paul's office as he would work on vocal parts, arrangements, and just write songs. Some nights it lasted all night 3 to 4 to 5 in the morning.

One day Gary asked Paul if he would be interested in producing him and he said yes. Gary was on cloud nine. So Paul, Dale, Joe and Gary were part of a team! Gary explains; what was discussed and said to be was that we were going to be a mini Motown. They would all help each other with whatever was needed. Background, voices, percussion, writing, or producing. Now this is where the tricky stuff comes in, Gary says. You remember Gary said, that Paul had been in New York many years before him, well he was being mentored by his manager/partner Bob Reno. So all the business savvy was in place for him in his head. Gary on the other hand was a singer who loves to write, produce, and just be in the studio, Gary said keep in mind because Paul was his manager, publisher, and producer. Being that he was his friend on top of all of this Gary thought that he had nothing to worry about. There was a schedule for everyone that Paul was recording at the time and they would each wait for their turn. It was fun, Gary said. Paul's door to his office was always opened. He would go in and ask Paul a question or what ever he needed to know. If something had a be done Paul secretary Lee, would do it for him. As they were all part of "Heather Productions". Gary would then miss his turn because they wanted him to go on the road as a road manager for a group called the "Peppermint Rainbow". This lasted about a month or so. So now Gary gets back in town, and his turn is up. They start to get songs sent over. Irwin Schuster brought over Neil Sedaka song called "Workin On A Groovy Thing". As soon as Gary heard it he liked it and he would like to sing and record it. The rest of the songs were not as easy because Paul and Gary did not agree on the style of music that Gary like to perform. Finally Larry Weiss came up and played "Sweet Laura Lee". Gary liked his version and demo, but Gary's version came out different. So finally they had four songs to go in and cut. Naturally Gary wanted "Workin On A Groovy Thing" as his A-Side well, Irwin heard it and went back and told the Fifth Dimension who needed a new single out and they had it on their album. They were told that if they were going to do that song it better be quick because Gary's was set to be released. They beat Gary by one week, it was a hit for them. Gary was told the lead singer could not record because of a throat problem, so that is why they pulled it off the album, instead of recording something new.

Cash Box — July 28, 1973

STEAM-BATH—Pictured (l to r standing) are Dale Frashuer, president of Steambath Productions; Eddie Deane, general professional manager of Burlington-Felsted Music; and Mimi Trepel, managing director of Burlington-Felsted, overlooking Garrett Strong, former lead singer-songwriter of pop-rock group Steam, signing a co-publishing, production contract between Steambath Music and Burlington Music. Scott's former group, Steam, had a number one hit a few years back entitled "Na Na Hey Hey (Kiss Him Goodbye)".

Question? But didn't his wife also sing lead?

Anyway it is back to the drawing board for Gary.

They wound up putting out "Sweet Laura Lee" which Gary was not crazy about leading with a ballad. Now they needed a B-side. The other two sides that were cut were just okay, per Gary, but the company thought they were good. Gary recalls on the day they were going into the studio Paul was a little short with him. All because Gary called in the morning to see if he was driving in or taking the train, he figured they could ride in together. So Gary told Dale that he waned to do a song that was written a few years back in an office they had over the bus terminal in Bridgeport. It was called "Kiss Him Goodbye". So Dale told him per Gary and the studio was booked for 7 PM. Gary explains to the readers; for those of you who think "NA NA" was recorded in Bridgeport, it was not! It was recorded at Mercury at 110 W. 57 street. Paul studio was not even built yet. They went into the studio. Paul made and eight bar loop of a drum track from one of Gary's sides called "Sugar" by Neil Sedaka. Then the layering process began. There is absolutely "NO GUITAR", NO BASS" on the record. What you hear is all piano and organ overdubs. Those strings on the piano were matted with tape to get a different tone. Vibes were put in and Gary played percussion on a board that they found on the bottom of a Leslie speaker that was delivered to them. Gary was tapping on the vinyl console and Paul said, let's do that, so we taped pieces of cloth around the tips of the drumsticks and Gary played the board, while Dale and Gary were in the control room of the studio as Paul was playing different parts trying to find pieces that worked. Gary would say to Dale, tell Paul to keep that part, which he did several times. Don't forget Gary said that Paul was a little cool towards him that night so this was The Only Way, Gary got the message to Paul from Dale. Warren Dewey, if he is still alive, can verify this, if he remembers. Now it is time to run over the vocal which Gary was singing in the control room. Paul had to hook all the NA NA, NA NA NA NA, NA NA NA, GOODBYE. So when Gary sang it he then added, "HEY, HEY, HEY" with it, at the PIANO with Paul, and thus it became the famous chant, that you hear to this very day 2012. Per Gary, now it was his turn to saying. They had just finished all the background parts and now Gary was pumped up, he rang it down to get levels and did it. Everything that you hear Gary sing as far as ad Libs came out of his head on the spot by 5 AM the record was mixed and it sounded just the way that you hear it on the radio, minus the mastering. Gary explains, so he goes home gets up hours later, the first thing he does is to listen to the mix and he likes it. Gary feels this may cause a problem, but he is told by Paul that he could put both records out because they were both his, seeing as how the company wanted the record split, meaning they did not want "NA NA" to be a B-Side. So now Gary said, he is happy. Now, two records out at the same time and he could perform both of them. Gary explains; again I have to back up a bit. Before the recordings were made Paul and Gary had a discussion about Gary putting a group together that he worked with at home.

Garrett Scott's star rising as singer, writer and producer

BY JIM KNIPPENBERG

If you aren't familiar with the name Garrett Scott, you soon will be.

No doubt you're familiar with his voice already. He was the lead voice on "Na, Na Hey, Hey, Kiss Him Goodbye," the Steam hit which has sold by now nearly a million and a half copies and is high up on the charts in something like 13 countries.

Soundings

But there's more of a story than that. Garrett Scott was in town two weeks ago and we had a chance to talk.

"Actually I never was with Steam," he said, "I just co-authored the songs on the album and performed on 'Na, Na'. My career is different."

Unfortunately his career is very different—and totally separate — from Steam. Garrett is a solo performer mainly, a writer secondly, and a producer after that.

"Right now," he said, "I'm working on getting a revue together. There will be seven pieces with a girl singer, trumpet, tenor sax, organ, guitar and drums. So far it's pretty much in the planning stage, only partially organized, but we're playing everything possible— funky Latin to commercial rock."

"The act," he continued, "is a visual as well as musical thing. Kind of a Sly/Jr. Walker thing. The musicians we have so far and those we're looking for are professionally trained people."

WISELY ENOUGH, Garrett is not aiming for any special group. Instead, he and his crew are playing music for people of all factions.

"Rather than alienating any specific group," he said, "we're just trying to play good stuff."

"The music we do," he went on, "is the good stuff others have done and then stylized to fit our act."

From this, they get a distinctive sound and familiarity at the same time.

You can hear the distinctive sound on "I'm Going To Give You All My Love," his first solo release, a commercial little number on the Mercury label. Of late, the record has been starting to take off on the top 40 stations.

Garrett Scott is 22 years old. He's been into music since he was 10 years old.

"It started with the drums when I was 10," he said. "I was a real musician on them. Since then, I've been into music for both fun and profit."

Currently, Garrett is doing a personal appearance tour. He's already been steps on the Mann Cuss show on the West Coast, Scene '76 in New York, and Up-Beat in Cleveland.

More important, he's making a round of personal appearances before live audiences.

"The tour," he commented, "is mainly on the college and the rock club circuit."

Garrett explains this...

NOW 3¢

FOR THE WEEK OF JAN. 11 thru JAN. 17

25 HOT HEAVIES

I NEED YOU
TO LOVE
WHEN I'M DEAD AND GONE

Week of December 13, 1969

This Wk Dec 13	Last Wk Dec 6		Wks. on Chart
1	4	NA NA HEY HEY KISS HIM GOODBYE Steam Featuring Garrett Scott — Fontana 1667	12
2	5	LEAVING ON A JET PLANE Peter, Paul & Mary — WB 7 Arts 7340	7
3	1	COME TOGETHER / SOMETHING Beatles — Apple 2654	10
4	6	FORTUNATE SON / DOWN ON THE CORNER Creedence Clearwater Revival — Fantasy 634	8
5	8	SOMEDAY WE'LL BE TOGETHER Supremes — Motown 1156	6
6	3	TAKE A LETTER MARIA R. B. Greaves — Atco 6714	10
7	9	HOLLY HOLY Neil Diamond — Uni 55175	7
8	2	AND WHEN I DIE Blood, Sweat & Tears — Columbia 4-45008	9
9	10	YESTER-ME YESTER-YOU YESTERDAY Stevie Wonder — Tamla 54188	8
10	21	RAINDROPS KEEP FALLIN' ON MY HEAD B. J. Thomas — Scepter 12265	7
11	12	BACKFIELD IN MOTION Mel & Tim — Bamboo 107	9
12	7	ELI'S COMING Three Dog Night — Dunhill 4215	10
13	14	BABY I'M FOR REAL Originals — Soul 35066	12
14	11	WEDDING BELL BLUES Fifth Dimension — Soul City 777	10
15	16	CHERRY HILL PARK Billy Joe Royal — Columbia 44902	7
16	17	HEAVEN KNOWS Grass Roots — Dunhill 4217	5
17	23	LA LA LA (IF I HAD YOU) Bobby Sherman — Metromedia 150	12
18		TELL ME... SMILE FOR ME	

This Wk	Last Wk		
33	41	I'LL HOLD OUT MY HAND The Clique — White Whale 332	
34	37	YOU'VE GOT TO PAY THE PRICE Gloria Taylor — Silver Fox 18	
35	42	WHOLE LOTTA LOVE Led Zeppelin — Atlantic 2690	
36	38	MIDNIGHT Sunny, Dore & Others (?)	
37	39	SEE RUBY FALL Johnny Cash — Columbia 45020	
38	49	EARLY IN THE MORNING Vanity Fare — Page One 21027	
39	47	JINGLE JANGLE Archies — Kirshner	
40	18	SUITE: JUDY BLUE EYES Crosby, Stills & Nash — Atlantic 2676	
41	48	AIN'T IT FUNKY NOW PT. 1 James Brown — King 6280	
42	28	MIND BODY & SOUL Flaming Ember — Hot Wax 6906	
43	50	DON'T LET LOVE HANG YOU UP Jerry Butler — Mercury 72991	
44	30	LOVE WILL FIND A WAY Jackie DeShannon — Imperial 66419	
45	40	RINGO Lorne Greene — Columbia	
46	43	ON THE ROCK OF THE BAY Sailcat — Capitol 933	
47	22	MAKE YOUR OWN KIND OF MUSIC Mama Cass — Dunhill 4214	
48	51	KOZMIC BLUES Janis Joplin — Columbia 45023	
49	52	GOIN' IN CIRCLES Friends of Distinction — RCA 74-0204	
50	91	VENUS Shocking Blue — Colossus 108	
51	73	WONDERFUL WORLD BEAUTIFUL PEOPLE Jimmy Cliff — A&M	
52	55	GET IT FROM THE BOTTOM The Steelers — Date	
53	54	SHINDIG TERRY	

Congratulations
by WESTERN UNION

B BPA211 AS PDF BRIDGEPORT CONN 17 31TFEST
GARRETH SCOTT (75 DLY)
CARE CREATIVE SLIPCOVERS 2338 MAIN ST BRIDGE

Carnegie Hall

57th Street & 7th Avenue, New York City, Box Office: CI 7-7460

गारिया Scott
P/W/A gary DeCATLO

Please examine your tickets before leaving the window.
No tickets exchanged or money refunded.
Not responsible for reservations call on box office.

Paul said to Gary, forget about those guys, if you need a group I will get you one right here in New York. Okay, back forward both records are just put out and they both start making some noise and start getting attention. Paul says to Gary the record company wants a group to go out promoting "NA NA". Gary said to Paul I don't have a group and beside you told me I could do both. Well, they want to group, Gary does not have a group, Paul told him to forget about the guys back home. Now Gary was starting to get into a real "funk". Then Bob comes in and says don't worry about it Gary we are going to work "Sweet Laura Lee" real hard and it will be a hit. They both made it seem to Gary like it would and could be done. Now Gary said he was starting to get depressed. He sees the amount of records coming just from our company and hardly any of them got airplay. Little by little "NA NA" kept climbing up the charts and "Sweet Laura Lee" was not doing bad but it did not get the WLS Chicago station and little by little it faded away. So here I am Gary said, and "Sweet Laura Lee" is Done Obviously they did not have the resources to bring a record home as they said they could. Gary kept telling them that you said I could do both records why can't I just go on the road with the group "Steam", do "NA NA" and a few other songs. After "NA NA's life is over, he said to Paul, I can go my way as Garrett Scott and they can continue as steam. Paul said NO! Now Gary said that he is really upset, depressed, and confused. Gary then called Bob Reno and asked to see him in his office. Dale came with him. Gary told Bob it was not right what was happening and I he wanted to go on the road with steam, as he had been saying to Paul. Bob told him it is fine, it would be okay. Gary felt much better and he went home for the night. The next day Paul tracked Gary down at his sister's house. He kept Gary on the phone four 1 1/2 hours, telling him it was a bad idea, it was not going to work. Gary said that he reached his breaking point, he finally had enough thinking about why Paul is doing this. Gary said to Paul forget it!, And just hung up. Gary expresses with great emotion; now I'm upset, depressed, confused, and pissed to think that Paul would do this to me. Paul became very cool towards Gary. Now he needed a B-side for the B-side that became an A-Side. Same scenario as "NA NA". A drum loop track and Gary saying yes that part is good and Dale telling Paul to keep it. Now they were ready for the lead vocal. Gary does the lead vocal and Paul tells him he does not like his vocal. So guess who does the vocal? Are you all starting to feel a pattern here? Gary gets into a discussion with Paul about the rest of the vocals. Gary said that this is his album, really because if it was not for "NA NA" there would be no album!

Paul says "No Way", "this is for Steams Album. He said to Gary, he wanted him to sing the rest of all the songs on the album and the singers from the road group would take credit like they did on the "NA NA Song". Gary immediately said "NO". He told Paul that "THIS IS MY VOICE, MY SOUND, THAT I CREATED". Paul had the attitude of "so what", that's no big deal. Gary said remember what the people did when they found out Milli Vinelli, was not singing their songs! The fans were not very happy. They literally ran over their CDs and cassettes with the steamroller. Obviously it was and still is a big deal to the fans! The acting group did an injustice to the song and a bad job at that! But as the acting group went out on tour the fans picked up on their deception and the group slowly faded away!

On December 6, 1969 "NA NA" was a # 1 HIT for weeks!

Gary told Paul he would not sing anything else on the album. Paul told Gary to sing demos so the lead singer can learn them. IMAGINE THAT! Gary refused, he did not want to be a part of this deception!

As they were writing and finishing up the songs for the album there was a big change in Paul. He wanted total control not a collaboration like with "NA NA". Plus his office door was no longer opened. He started wearing sunglasses and dimmed the lights in his office. Gary recalls that you had to either knock on the door or ask his secretary to ring him, to see or talk to him. He said Paul also started wearing suede pants and puff sleeved shirts. Gary came in one day to find a note taped to the office door that was for Dale, Joe, and him to write in. The note read: This Office Is For Dale Frashuer and Joe Messina. No one else is allowed in ! Gary, to say the least, was taken back by the note and very frustrated. Gary after seeing this then told Paul that he wanted out of this contract. Paul said okay, he will have one drawn up. The contract would say that Gary would no longer be involved with future Steam recordings. But, that Gary would still be paid for the songs that he had written and still received his share. Paul had a friend with them who came up from Cleveland and had a partner with whom he had a management company. One day Paul said to Gary that this might be something he should consider. So Gary said okay and signed on with them. Not knowing all the time that they were under Paul's umbrella! Yes, Paul's umbrella! Gary then had John and Mike his new managers look at the release and they assured him that it was fine. He signed the contract and he came to find out years later, there was a controversy over the way the contract was read. Gary only made around $15,000 as an artist from "NA NA". Think about that Gary says, he was told that the records sold over 6 1/2 million copies and that was some time ago! The last time Gary was paid was in 1974. Here we are in 2012 he says, 43 years later, I say 43 years later.

When Gary's "NA NA disco version came out he was invited to several discos. He would mingle and meet people and in some cases be a judge to a disco dance off, while "NA NA was playing.

I say 43 years later and the song "NA NA "is still being played in films, commercials, sporting events, and still being recorded. Gary had not spoken to Paul in many years. He was told as the years went by that they were booking several groups around the country as steam. Gary said he did not know but it makes sense that if he was with the road group singing the lead as Garrett Scott, it would have been hard to have other groups on the road when Gary would be known as the "Lead Singer". What Gary would like to have the readers and the public, Internet, understand and think about is that Paul was his manager, publisher, producer, and supposedly his "Friend". As a manager, his duty was to guide you and show and teach you how you can be the best you can be. Think of them as say for example a lawyer, a doctor, a stockbroker, etc. If these professionals tell you something is right or wrong, you take their word for it. If you do not feel they are right you should not be with them. This is what Gary did with Paul. He believed in him, and that he would not, and could not, do anything that was exactly happening to him. Boy was Gary so wrong! Gary asks, please do not get me wrong, I am not trying to take away from Paul and his accomplishments. He was a hard worker and he had several records. He was a self-taught man. Gary points out a few things that he has seen on the Internet from people who think they know the "NA NA STORY". Well they do not! Remember Gary says, I am speaking of all my experiences with Paul. He was a different person when you did business with him. And the Internet people say, that Gary did not like "NA NA" and that he did not want to go on the road. "THAT IS AN OUTRIGHT LIE"! You can ask anyone Gary says, who knows him and they can tell you it is not true. Gary says he is sure Dale's wife Mary, would speak on his defense. Another thing on the Internet is how all of Paul's records were hits and all of Gary's bombed out. They did not bomb out Gary can show you the charts. They were all getting airplay and great reviews at that! Gary does not think that is fair, when people compare his five recordings to Paul's 100 recordings. Think of the ratio here. Also, for the record, no one knows that Paul had the first "Candida" recording which was not liked. Hank Medress recorded the song with the same people and had a hit. Their names were, "Tony Orlando and Dawn". He also had a recording of "The Worst That Can Happen" by Johnny Maestro and the Crests. Again it was not liked. Wes Ferrell recorded the song which Johnny and had the hit. Paul also made about seven recordings with groups and single artist in the same format as "NA NA". Gary says, "I guess to prove that he could do it again without me this time". None of the recordings did anything, not even airplay. He also had a chance to sign Michael McDonald. Irv Azoff came to Paul's office with a cassette of Michael. Gary was in Paul's office at the time and he played it for him. Gary said to him, "what are you going to do with this Kid"?. Paul said, nothing, I don't know what to do with him. Gary said to Paul put him on tape that's all you need to do. Gary knew that Michael had it and he tried to validate that with Paul. That is when Gary realized that he was out of his element.

Singing live is very different from singing in a studio Gary says. In a studio, you punch in and out, do other things over until you feel it is right. On stage you have One Shot to do your Best! So you put all your heart and soul and energy into that vocal. Paul had a habit of breaking your concentration by stopping you for not saying a word properly or phrasing it the way he thought it should be or for any other reason. Gary did not know if Paul was thinking about how he would sing it. He could not and still cannot figure it out. Gary says I am sure he did not do that when recording Harry Chapin or REO speed wagon. If the producer continually stops the singer, while recording in essence he is chipping away at his confidence unless of course, the person cannot sing to begin with or he just had a problem with that person. How frustrating the situation was. Every song Gary would do as a live performer he would bring up to Paul and say that he would like to record it. He always said NO to him. Gary wanted to record "Sad Girl", it was later redone and became a hit. The same for "Hey Girl Knock On Wood" and "Tell It Like It Is". He said to Paul one day here is the type of song I would like to do. Gary then played the "Bread" single for him. "I Wanna Make It With You", Paul told Gary that is an awful song. The guitars are out of time. Okay now, "Bread" went on to have hit after hit after hit! Gary with great emotion asks the reader: "I would like who ever reads this to think about all I have said and to go on the Internet, punch in my name, and read what is there". After 43 years of people constantly saying, "Oh I know so-and-so, he played on the record"! Or people ask me, Gary do you still see any of the guys in the group? "PLEASE" once and for all "THERE WAS NO GROUP"!!! "NA NA was made by Paul, Dale, and myself, Gary says it was my record, and I will never get all of those years back that I could have performed this song and felt the way I feel now when I perform and sing it today! Gary says, "but if you see and hear me, you will know that it was me all along and I was and still am the singer of "NA NA HEY HEY KISS HIM GOODBYE"—Gary explains to me with much emotion: It was not easy for me to watch the road group lip sync to "NA NA" on American Bandstand, no less, while they displayed a GOLD RECORD in front of Dick Clark productions. How would you all feel I asked"?

When Gary was in California a year or so after "NA NA" visiting his father he somehow went to lunch with Bob Reno in Beverly Hills. During lunch Bob said to Gary, don't be mad at Paul, he is a really good kid. Paul had a way of sabotaging some of his records. Imagine that! He was one of the first to make it to # 1 on the charts from our area. But Gary and a few others noticed that if he did a record with someone he knew some part of the puzzle was not there. It seemed as if Paul did not want anyone to outshine his success. Especially someone from the same area. There was a drastic change in Paul after "NA NA". It was as if he started to believe and live his press clippings. Gary explains that those of us who did business with him saw a totally different side of him unless of course you were Female!

Gary explains this with much passion: I do not want to beat this into the ground, but I just would like to make you understand why I feel the way I do. If "NA NA" was so worthless, just a throwaway, as Paul said in many interviews, why then could it not have been put as my B-Side which is what it was anyways. It says in many articles that the record company felt I knew that it should be on its own. Who are they, you ask? Well, Bob Reno was vice president and also Paul's partner and manager at Mercury records. Many people have put out records with two good sides. I personally have found several B-Sides that I like more than A-Sides. Maybe all my experiences with Paul would give people enough nerve to come out and tell their story of what had been done to them in doing business with Paul. He was not a bad person but to do business with him, he then became a shark! Gary knew all of this for a fact because over the years several people came up to him and told him of their stories.

A couple of years later Gary received a call from a guy named Ralph who worked on Channel 13, PBS station. He had a very similar request for Gary to be involved in a show with other talents. Again they did not come to be but Ralph introduced Gary to Charlie Rosenay, which Gary thanks him for.

Several years later Gary received a call from a disc jockey named Stormin Norman who by the way is a favorite DJ on the air at WEBE 108. Stormin asked Gary if he would be interested in being involved in the show with other Connecticut talents like Felix Cavaliere of the Rascals and a few other singers and great artists. Gary said yes he would be glad and honored to perform. No one would commit due to several reasons unfortunately so this never happened for him.

In 1981 Gary was out with his cousin Gene Piccorillo having a drink at a bar in Westport Connecticut. There was a hair salon right above it. This is where Annette worked. She came down to the bar with a few co-workers to have a drink before going home. That is where Gary and Annette bumped into each other. Gary recalls, they said hi, had a short but nice conversation, and said goodbye. Annette was off to Canada for a hair Expo. They did not meet up again till about a month later at the same bar. She gave Gary her number and they talked. He then asked her if she would like to join him for a large picnic at Sherwood Island in Westport. She said yes, she came down, and they spent the day together. Gary and Annette started to see each other on a regular basis. After about a year or so Annette was at Gary's house more than her own apartment. Gary suggested to her they move in together.

Their feelings for one another grew and they wanted to spend as much time with one another as they could. They both made a plan and made it happen. As time went by Annette wanted to get married and start a family. Gary was not ready at that time. He still wanted to pursue his music career, as nonexisting as it was, he said Gary felt that if you made that commitment, there was a chance he could be on the road and not at home with his family. So they waited. Gary said that it was very stressful for them because Annette wanted it and she just did not want to wait anymore. As the years went by Gary realized his career was pretty much dead, he was not getting younger, and it was time to move forward. He loved Annette and wanted to begin a life together Gary and Annette finally married. In 1990 on Christmas Day they had their first daughter Jenna. Gary was 48 at the time. Gary recalls that special day; he said the nurses brought Jenna to them in a Christmas stocking. She was so tiny he said, and she was ours.! Jenna was a colicky baby so she cried for the first three months of her life. It was not fun Gary said, but Annette and I pulled it together. Annette and Gary decided it was time to sell the house and move to a different area, different home, where the schools were better. So in 1992 they sold the home and moved to Shelton, Connecticut. Annette was pregnant with their second child, another girl, and her name is Leah. Leah was born in January of 1992. So now we had our family Gary said. Most people would be happy and contented with this life and I was and still am but, "NA NA" kept popping up in his life for various reasons. Gary knew in his heart that there was much unfinished business with the "NA NA" song and its life. He knew that he could never be happy without being able to show people that he had made some decent recordings and his contribution with "NA NA". After a while he said to me you start to think that you just were not good enough to make it in the music business. He only had a handful of people who were genuinely sincere in wishing him well. He also realized that everyone has their own problems to deal with, so we tried very hard to work through it all. Some days are good for Gary, others are not. He's dealing with a hearing problem. Gary's passion for music and his songs and the story behind "NA NA" is his goal. And through it all he will persevere to continue with what he loves to do and to validate the story behind "NA NA"!

Gary closes his story with me with unanswered questions. He told me that he wants the readers and the people out there on the Internet to know what he had to go through with the whole "NA NA" episode.

1. Why couldn't "NA NA" be a B-side?
   If it was such a piece of crap as Paul called it!

2. Why couldn't he go on the road with the first group?
   They could have launched two careers!

3. Why was Gary told to step away from the group and musicians that he worked with?

4. Why didn't Paul get Gary the backup group that he said he would?

5. Why was Gary told he could promote both records when they were both put out?

6. Why was Gary told not to tell anyone that he was the lead vocalist on "NA NA" when Gary did the TV shows?

If Paul was really a friend he would have made sure that Gary was identified as the lead singer of "NA NA".

HE HAD OVER 40 YEARS TO DO IT!

Artist's that recorded "NA NA"

- ❖ Dion and the Belmonts
- ❖ The Nylons
- ❖ Gary Puckett
- ❖ Axxis
- ❖ Supremes
- ❖ Jeronimo Cosmic Blues
- ❖ Star Flyer
- ❖ Bananarama (1983) Top 10 Hit in England
- ❖ Smash One Band
- ❖ Hugo Montenegro
- ❖ Fancy
- ❖ Master Voice L.I. P.M.
- ❖ Christina DeBarge "Goodbye"
- ❖ Robbie Rob (Bad Boys Brothers)

Movies that used the "NA NA" song

❖ Remember the Titans

❖ Eddie

❖ Raising Helen

Gary's Songs

- ❖ Na Na Hey Hey Kiss Him Goodbye

  Co-Wrote & Recorded

- ❖ I Fall In Love Again

  Wrote & Recorded

- ❖ Can't Help But Love Her

  Wrote & Recorded

- ❖ We Milked It

  Wrote & Recorded

- ❖ Tomorrow is Another Day

  Wrote & Recorded

Gary's Songs

- ❖ Something in the Way

  Wrote & Recorded
- ❖ I'm Gonna Give You All My Love

  Wrote & Recorded
- ❖ Workin on a Groovy Thing

  Recorded

Gary

I personally would like to take this opportunity to thank you along with all of your fans for your contribution to the music industry for Na Na Hey Hey Kiss Him Goodbye and all of your other Recordings that you have written and sang. You have touched all of our lives with your music and we are forever grateful to you!

Mary R. Scinto

20011618R00074

Made in the USA
Lexington, KY
16 January 2013